KT-134-008

POCKET STUDY SKILLS

*Series Editor: **Kate Williams**, Oxford Brookes University, UK*
Illustrations by Sallie Godwin

For the time-pushed student, the *Pocket Study Skills* pack a lot of advice into a little book. Each guide focuses on a single crucial aspect of study giving you step-by-step guidance, handy tips and clear advice on how to approach the important areas which will continually be at the core of your studies.

Published

14 Days to Exam Success
Blogs, Wikis, Podcasts and More
Brilliant Writing Tips for Students
Completing Your PhD
Doing Research
Getting Critical
Planning Your Essay
Planning Your PhD
Reading and Making Notes
Referencing and Understanding Plagiarism
Reflective Writing
Report Writing
Science Study Skills
Studying with Dyslexia
Success in Groupwork
Time Management
Writing for University

Pocket Study Skills
Series Standing Order
ISBN 978–0230–21605–1
(outside North America only)

You can receive future titles in this series as they are published by placing a standing order. Please contact your bookseller or, in case of difficulty, write to us at the address below with your name and address, the title of the series and the ISBN quoted above.

Customer Services Department, Macmillan Distribution Ltd, Houndmills, Basingstoke, Hampshire RG21 6XS England

POCKET STUDY SKILLS

Michelle Reid

REPORT WRITING

palgrave
macmillan

First published 2012 by
PALGRAVE MACMILLAN

Palgrave Macmillan in the UK is an imprint of Macmillan Publishers Limited, registered in England, company number 785998, of Houndmills, Basingstoke, Hampshire RG21 6XS.

Palgrave Macmillan in the US is a division of St Martin's Press LLC, 175 Fifth Avenue, New York, NY 10010.

Palgrave Macmillan is the global academic imprint of the above companies and has companies and representatives throughout the world.

Palgrave® and Macmillan® are registered trademarks in the United States, the United Kingdom, Europe and other countries

ISBN: 978-0-230-37655-7

This book is printed on paper suitable for recycling and made from fully managed and sustained forest sources. Logging, pulping and manufacturing processes are expected to conform to the environmental regulations of the country of origin.

A catalogue record for this book is available from the British Library.

A catalog record for this book is available from the Library of Congress.

Printed in China

Contents

Acknowledgements

Thank you to the students I work with at the University of Reading who discuss their report writing concerns and insights, and who continually give me new ideas. I am very grateful to my colleague Kim Shahabudin whose research into report writing for the LearnHigher CETL helped me understand reports as a genre and set of writing styles. Special thanks to students and staff at the University of Reading who kindly shared examples of reports from their subjects and allowed me to include them in the book, especially Peter Cook, John Harris, David Kirk and Kathy Pain. Many thanks to Kate Williams for her expert guidance, advice … and all those cups of tea. Thanks also to Suzannah Burywood and the editorial and production teams at Palgrave Macmillan for their creativity and support. Thank you to Sallie Godwin for her fabulous illustrations that make the book come to life. Finally, a big thank you to Inigo for being brilliant.

Introduction

Business reports … lab reports … research reports … there are many different kinds of reports that you might have to write as part of your university course. This is because the report format is a useful and widely accepted way of structuring information.

Knowing how to structure a report and get the information in the right place can cause concerns:

- Which section should this go in?
- How do I lay out my report?
- What goes in the discussion?
- What headings does a business report have?

This book answers these questions by showing you how a report structure can be a communication tool as opposed to an imprisoning set of rules. If you consider the purpose of your report and the needs of your readers, you can be confident that your structure will fulfil these needs, and each section of your report will do the correct job.

This book demonstrates the purpose and readership of reports, how to find the information your readers need, the role that each section plays in communicating this information, how to present your information visually ... and how to communicate all this concisely!

Most professions (and university subjects) have their own kinds of reports, so knowing how to write them well is valuable at university and beyond.

Reports are formally structured and communicate the findings of an investigation in a clear, logical way.

Your investigation may be a scientific experiment, a site visit, a series of observations, research into a process or procedure … but whatever different types of investigation you do as part of your course, you will need to *report*

- what you did
- how you did it
- what you found out
- why your findings are important.

The content and structure of your report are determined by the needs of your **audience** and the **purpose** of your report … but how do you know who your audience is and what they want?

Read the brief!

Reports normally have a brief, or a set of instructions, telling you the requirements of your investigation.

In a work situation the brief may be set by your clients or your manager, and they expect you to follow it! At university your brief is most likely set by your tutor ... and they also expect you to follow it!

You will get the crucial information you need from reading your brief carefully:

The main purpose is a feasibility study.

Investigate the feasibility of using wind power to generate some of the electricity for the new halls of residence on the Central Campus.

Identify different ways to use wind power to generate electricity. Develop a set of criteria for evaluating these methods of power generation for a hall of residence. Make recommendations on the feasibility of using wind power at the new hall for the Campus Facilities Manager to take to the next Planning and Policy Board meeting.

Identify … develop … make recommendations – these are the things your audience wants included in the report.

Note that you are asked to define criteria for evaluating the methods of wind power generation yourself, so you need to define how you are judging 'feasibility' – what would your audience consider the most important factors making wind power feasible?

– cost effectiveness?
– efficiency?
– reliability?

Your main audience is the Campus Facilities Manager, but you have a secondary audience, the Planning and Policy Board – so the recommendations you make need to be suitable for the Manager to take to this meeting.

Even a short brief contains a lot of information about what you are expected to do.

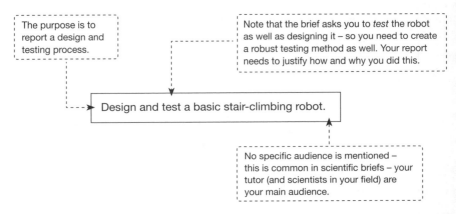

The purpose is to report a design and testing process.

Note that the brief asks you to *test* the robot as well as designing it – so you need to create a robust testing method as well. Your report needs to justify how and why you did this.

Design and test a basic stair-climbing robot.

No specific audience is mentioned – this is common in scientific briefs – your tutor (and scientists in your field) are your main audience.

Your brief tells you about the investigation you are carrying out, but you also need to know the essential requirements of your assignment, such as:

- word count
- format
- referencing style
- deadline for handing in.

In addition to this, **read your assessment criteria** – these will give you valuable information about what you need to demonstrate in your report and the 'learning outcomes' you are expected to fulfil.

Who is the audience?

A report is a piece of *informative* writing, which means it has an intended audience who want to find things out from reading your report.

Your brief or assignment description should tell you who your intended audience is, and this has an important influence on the content of your report; you need to tailor the information to suit the needs of your audience.

Reports about the same subject written for different audiences would have a very different content and tone.

> Write a report on the intended care plan for a severely disabled child.

How might your report differ if you were writing it for …

▶ the family of the child?
▶ the community care worker helping to implement the plan?
▶ the Social Services department overseeing the plan?
▶ the Disability Living Allowance coordinator judging whether the plan should be financed?

> Write a report on the habitat and population of rare great crested newts on the site of a disused factory.

How might your report differ if you were writing it for...

A national conservation charity...

A development company wanting to build a new supermarket...

The town council wanting to improve employment...

Lawyers acting for the factory owners...

A local shop owners' group...

An audience has a vested interest in the information being reported and motivations for wanting the investigation conducted. As a report writer, you need to take these needs into consideration.

This is why, even though your brief is set by your tutor, they may ask you to write for an imaginary client or a professional situation. In this scenario, you need to consider who will use the information that you are reporting and how they will use it – for example, will your recommendations be passed on to a secondary audience or used to advise clients or managers? What will be relevant and useful for these audiences?

If your main audience is your tutor, they still want to know that you can report the findings of your investigation in a logical and relevant way, relating them to the overall purpose of the investigation.

What is the purpose?

As a report is a piece of informative writing, it not only has an audience who wants to be informed, it also has a *purpose* – a reason for wanting the information.

What do your readers want to find out from your report?
How will they be reading your report?
Why will they be reading what you are reporting?

Often, the information in reports will be *acted upon* by your readers in some way. The information in different reports may have the purpose of advising, persuading or recommending the readers to do something.

You are asked to analyse whether regular exercise helps people manage their depression, and present the report to an audience of counsellors and doctors.

The purpose of the report is to inform the audience about whether this potential aid in the management of depression is supported by sufficient evidence.

The counsellors and doctors will want to know whether they should be recommending more regular exercise to their clients and patients based on your analysis of the evidence.

So your report needs to give clear guidance on whether the evidence suggests there are benefits to people with depression, and to what extent counsellors and doctors should act on this information.

But part of persuading an audience is being able to anticipate any scepticism they may have about the evidence you present. For example, the doctors and counsellors may raise the objection, *how* do we encourage our depressed patients to start exercising? You have to take this into account – just a brief acknowledgement of their concerns may make them more receptive to your message.

You may be thinking that the concept of 'purpose' doesn't apply in the same way to reports on scientific experiments, but the principles of audience and purpose still apply. As a scientist, your audience is your tutor (and fellow scientists in your field) and your purpose may be to test your hypotheses. Based on the analysis of your findings, you may make recommendations for further research to fill gaps in your findings or to make them more robust.

If your brief asks you to make recommendations based on the information in your report, it is important that you make these clearly, and that they don't get lost in the body of your conclusion. Recommendations serve a different purpose to a conclusion: a conclusion summarises *why* your findings are important, and recommendations say *what* your readers should do about this.

What does your audience know already?

Not only do you need to consider the needs of your audience and what they want to find out from your report, you also have to take into account their background – what information do they already have? You don't want to repeat unnecessary information since a report has to be as concise and as relevant to your readers as possible (and you also have a word count to stick to!)

In a work situation, including information that your readers already know will undermine your authority and make your readers less receptive to your message. On your university course, your tutors want to see that you can be selective and make judgements about what is relevant. Your marking criteria will probably include something about relevance or suitability of the information.

> *The introduction to a lab report shouldn't be a long historical summary of all the experiments done in the field. The methods and findings of most older experiments have now been surpassed.*
> *(Food Science and Nutrition lecturer)*

> *A main problem with my students' surveying reports is they spend too long describing the client's house – but the client already knows what colour their own door is ... get to the interesting information more quickly.*
> *(Real Estate and Planning lecturer)*

> *Demonstrating an understanding of the client's problem is important. It shows the students know what they are talking about, but I always ask: What is new about this? What insights are you giving me? How does your interpretation of my problem give me confidence that you're going to provide me with solutions?*
> *(International Marketing lecturer)*

How are reports read?

A report is an act of communication, so it is helpful to understand how your audience will read your report.

When marking your report, your tutor is likely to read it all the way through from beginning to end, as they need to see how you have fulfilled the marking criteria.

However, reports are not normally read in such a linear way. A reader is likely to go straight to the sections that they think will give them the information they need, and then make decisions about whether to read the rest of the report based on this.

Reports are about finding relevant information easily. Each section of a report does a specific job (as shown in Chapter 3), so the structure of the report signals to the reader where they can find the information they want easily and quickly.

Research into how managers read reports (cited by University of Reading 2008a) showed that they were most likely to read in order:

1 the abstract or summary
2 the introduction
3 the conclusions
4 the findings
5 the appendices.

The way that managers read reports shows that the smaller sections of a report, like the abstract and conclusions, have an important role to play in helping your audience get the information they need. It is worth spending time making sure these sections are accurate because they act as your 'shop window', showing what your report contains and why your readers should care about this.

How are reports written?

Just as reports are not read in order from beginning to end, it is likely that you are not going to *write* your report in a linear way.

This is because a report is an account of an investigation that you have conducted … and investigations rarely happen in a linear, well-ordered manner!

Any investigation or piece of research is an iterative process: you start out in a certain direction (for example by making a plan, doing background reading or a pilot study) then, as a result of your initial findings, you often go back and change your original ideas, refining and developing them. An investigative journey often involves detours and loops before you fully work out where you want to go.

A report is an account of this investigative journey, but it imposes an artificial logic on it. Although you may have gone down diversions or looped back in your investigation, your report leads your readers through clearly, in an accepted formal order. Although each investigation is different and takes a different path, the structure of a report gives a familiar order to the information – we know what to expect, what we are going to find in each section, and what job that section does.

your investigation
journey

your report

Some sections of a report, like the **abstract** and **introduction**, give important context and summaries of the investigation, so can only really be written (or redrafted) at the end, when you have a clear idea of what you did and where you ended up.

Other sections of a report, like the **results** and **discussion**, are dependent on you finding out information or doing practical work, so you need to do this before you can write them up.

The **methods**, or descriptions of what you did, are something that you probably have to work out in advance (you need to know roughly what you are going to do before you can do it). It is also more descriptive and straightforward to write, so is likely to be a section that you can write first.

Differences between reports and essays

A report is a piece of informative writing with a specific audience and purpose; it is a distinct 'genre' or type of writing, and so it has a different style, features and conventions to other forms of writing that you might do as part of your course.

It is easier to see how a report is a distinct genre of writing if we compare it to another common genre of academic writing – the essay.

Reports	Essays
Purpose	
An account of an investigation	An answer to a question
Need to focus on the brief or the specific investigation set	Often has a broader scope – need to interpret and define the question
Reports what you have done and what you found out	Discusses an issue or point of academic contention
Makes recommendations supported by appropriate (referenced) evidence	Makes a coherent argument supported by appropriate (referenced) evidence
Audience	
Written for a specific audience established in the brief (e.g. a client, manager etc.) but your lecturer is also your audience	Not usually written for a specific audience (apart from your lecturer)
Format	
Formally structured with headings and sub-headings and bullet points	Continuous prose in paragraphs but usually with no headings or bullet points
Contains diagrams, tables, figures	Does not usually contain diagrams, tables, figures
Style	
Written in an appropriate style for each section (e.g. descriptive style for methods, analytical style for discussion)	Written in a single, discursive style throughout

These differences between reports and essays are generalised – some lecturers have different preferences, for example, encouraging the use of sub-headings in essays to break up the text. Always check with your individual assignment criteria first and if in doubt, ask.

You can get an idea of the different scope and intention of essays and reports by comparing these report briefs and essay questions:

Report briefs

> Based on your recent placement, compile a case report for a client, providing evidence for how you have taken issues of social injustice into account in their care plan.

> Investigate the conservation measures needed to ensure the correct preservation of human remains at the new dig site at Silbury Hill.

Essay questions

> The most important role of a social worker is to combat social injustice – discuss.

> What challenges are posed by the study of human remains for the reconstruction of past social organisation?

If you are not sure whether your assignment should be written as a report, essay or in another format, check your assignment guidelines and if you are still not sure, ask your tutor – selecting the wrong type of assignment format will definitely lose marks.

Types of reports

As reports are a useful and well-organised way of presenting information, they are found in many different professions and academic disciplines, ranging from the sciences, business and management, to health and social care.

Compare the basic outline structure of a science lab report and a business report:

In the first year of my Animal Science course we had to write field reports, lab reports and business reports!

(2nd year Animal Science student)

Science lab report
- Abstract
- Introduction
- Methods and materials
- Results
- Discussion
- Conclusions
- References

Business report
- Title page
- Executive summary
- Table of contents
- Introduction
- Discussion
- Conclusions
- Recommendations
- References
- Appendices

There is a similar logic and progression to both reports, even though some of the individual sections are different or have different names. This is because they have to serve the different needs and purposes of their readers – for example, this business report doesn't have a 'methods' section as the readers want to know what was found out and what to do about it; they are less interested in *how* the investigation was conducted. In contrast, the lab report has a methods and materials section because an important aspect of a scientific investigation is the rigour and repeatability of how it was done.

With all these different types of report – how can you know what you are supposed to do and what type of report is required?

Always start from the brief or instructions you are given. If your lecturers want you to follow specific conventions for your reports, they should let you know – so check your course handbook (paper or online) or ask.

Before you embark on your investigation, define your task:

What am I being asked to do?	Note …
What does the brief tell me about my investigation?	
Are there specific things that I need to include in the report?	

Who am I writing for?	
Who is my audience?	
What do they want to find out?	
What do they know already?	
How will they use the information?	
Are there secondary audiences who will see my report too?	

Why am I being asked to do it?	
Why is the report being written – what am I being asked to find out?	
Is the purpose of the report to inform, test, persuade, advise, recommend …?	
Have I been asked to make specific recommendations based on my findings?	

How does my audience want the information presented?	
What is the word count?	
What guidance have I been given on structure, format and layout?	
What style of referencing is required?	
Do I need to submit it electronically or in paper copy?	

When does my audience want the report?	
When is the deadline?	

Aims and objectives

Sometimes your investigation calls for you to establish your 'aims and objectives' – particularly for longer reports or dissertations. People often get aims and objectives confused and find it hard to distinguish between them. This is not surprising as major dictionaries usually define them as meaning the same thing.

However, in the context of a report:

- The aims are the overarching things you want to achieve.
- The objectives describe in more detail *how* you are going to achieve them.

By asking you to identify aims and objectives, your tutor wants you to break down and define your task more clearly.

For example, take the following brief:

> Investigate whether the university should create more alcohol-free social spaces on campus.

This is a very broad brief, so establishing aims and objectives can help give your investigation a more concrete focus.

Brief	Aims (what you want to achieve)	Objectives (how you will achieve it)
Investigate whether the university should create more alcohol-free social spaces on campus.	1 Establish whether there is student demand for more alcohol-free social spaces on campus.	(a) Observe how frequently and for what purpose the existing alcohol-free café bar is used by students.
		(b) Assess students' opinions on opportunities for alcohol-free socialising – including their health concerns and views on UK drinking culture.
	2 Identify whether creating more alcohol-free social spaces would be cost effective for the university.	(a) Evaluate the current profit/loss of the existing alcohol-free café bar.
		(b) Conduct a cost–benefit analysis for alternative sizes, locations and designs of alcohol-free social space on campus.

Even if you don't have to create specific aims and objectives as part of your report, you still need to identify **what you want to find out** and **how you are going to find that out** before you can go any further with your investigation.

What do you need to find out?

You have to clearly identify the problem and break it down into specific steps in order to find the information that your readers want.

If you are not sure where to start ... ask **SO WHAT?**

This question forces you to think about:

▶ So what ... does the audience see as the key issue or problem?
▶ So what ... are your audience's key concerns about the issue or problem (why do they care)?

Objectives	• Your objectives have to enable you to achieve your aims.
Aims	• Your aims have to fulfil the requirements of your brief.
Brief	• Your report has to answer your brief.

When supervising any of my students, from first years to PhDs, I always ask them 'So what?'... it makes them link back to the real world and the possible applications of their experiment.
(Head of Food Science)

- So what … will your audience do with the information you gather?
- So what … do you need to find out to provide your audience with information to answer their problem?

Imagine you have been given the following brief:

> Examine whether luxury brand cosmetics companies should adopt online viral marketing strategies.

SO WHAT?

So what does the audience see as the key issue or problem?

- New technologies may enable luxury cosmetic companies to reach new customers, or reach existing customers more effectively. Do luxury cosmetic companies need to take advantage of this trend?

So what are your audience's key concerns about the issue or problem (why do they care)?

- If luxury cosmetic companies don't keep developing their marketing strategies then rival companies could use these strategies more effectively.

So what will your audience do with the information you gather?

- Use the information to help decide their marketing strategy. Make decisions about the risks and benefits of adopting an online viral marketing campaign.

So what do you need to find out to provide your audience with information to answer their problem?

▶ What types of online viral marketing strategies are there?
▶ Who are the target consumers of luxury cosmetic companies?
▶ How do these consumers use the internet and how do they perceive online marketing?
▶ Which online viral marketing strategies would be most suited to reaching these target consumers?
▶ Will using these strategies benefit the cosmetic companies?
▶ What are the risks of not using these strategies?

Asking 'so what' has a dual purpose – it makes you consider the implications of what you are trying to investigate, and then, based on that, you can decide what you should find out.

How will you find this information out?

Once you have identified what you are trying to find out, you need to consider how you will gather this information. This will involve considering the *methods* you will use.

The methods you choose need to be fit for purpose and suitable for answering your aims and objectives, or your research questions.

In general, the methods you use can be divided into:

- **Primary research:** you collect original data first hand by doing experiments, interviews, surveys, focus groups, case studies etc.
- **Secondary research:** you find and analyse data that has already been collected by someone else – for example, reviewing existing literature or analysing existing statistics.

Many types of report you do at university will involve a combination of both primary and secondary research, for example background reading (secondary research) to put the investigation you are conducting (primary research) into context.

The research you do can be further divided into:

- **Qualitative research:** gauging people's feelings, attitudes or behaviours – for example, interviews, focus groups or case studies. This usually involves asking open-ended or semi-structured questions.
- **Quantitative research:** testing hypotheses by gathering numerical data or data that can be turned into numbers to be analysed – for example, measuring specific variables, or questionnaires with multiple choice answers. This usually involves creating standardised questions that provide numerically measurable answers.

Imagine you are asked to write a report investigating the question: *Does the current university education system provide good value for money for students?*

The idea of 'value for money' is complex and some of the research you need to do will be qualitative and some will be quantitative:

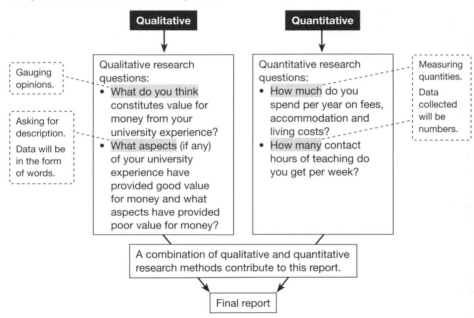

For more on the differences between qualitative and quantitative research and their relative advantages and disadvantages see Analyse This!!! at www.learnhigher.ac.uk/analysethis/index.html

It is likely that for many of the reports you are asked to write at university, your lecturer or tutor will give you an indication of the methods you are expected to use. Sometimes you are set report assignments specifically to enable you to learn certain methods (e.g. lab reports).

For longer projects and dissertations where you have to set your own research questions, you will be expected to apply what you have learned throughout your course to decide on the most appropriate methods to use.

For more on different research methods and how to find your data see Thomas G (2011) *Doing Research* in this series.

My university librarian showed me how to locate company reports and government statistics online. (3rd year Business and Management student)

When deciding how to find out the information you need to write your report, start from what you want to find out, then consider these questions:

- Does the information already exist somewhere?
- Has someone else researched it, and how can I get hold of this information?
- Do I need to conduct my own research to find the information?
- Will I need to gauge people's beliefs and opinions, or gather numerical data and test hypotheses?

Planning your time

Some element of working out *how* you intend to find out the information should also include *how long* you have to find this information.

A key part of conducting any investigation is planning your time. Trying to estimate how long stages in an investigation will take can be unpredictable and difficult … and in an ideal world there is always one more book you could read, or one more person you could interview.

A better strategy is to start with what is fixed and limited – the amount of time you have.

- Start with your assignment deadline and work backwards.
- Break your investigation into main stages and allot a certain amount of time for each stage.
- Set your own interim deadlines for when you will start and (more importantly) stop each stage and move on to the next one.
- Build in some contingency time (especially if you have to rely on other people responding when collecting your data).

For example:

Task	Get brief, start thinking of ideas		Start background reading	Start info gathering; Start writing methods	Finish background reading		Write introduction; Finish info gathering.; Finish methods. Start writing results	Continue analysing results	Write discussion and conclusion	Write abstract. Proof-reading and final checks. **HAND IN**
Week	1	2	3	4	5	6	7	8	9	10

If you are doing lab reports, you will probably be writing them up over a much shorter period of time, say 1 to 2 weeks, but you will be expected to do less background reading and of course you'll have already conducted the investigative part in class.

For more on how to break up a report into stages and create an assignment plan see ASK: Assignment Survival Kit from the University of Kent www.kent.ac.uk/uelt/ai/ask/index.php

I start writing up my lab reports as soon as we've come out of the practical – the methods and procedures are fresh in my mind. (2nd year Chemistry student)

Recording your findings

The way you record your findings depends on what you are investigating, but a good basic check is: Will you be able to find everything you need again and make sense of it all when you come to compile your final draft?

Recording your findings is about more than just being organised; it helps you start to structure and make sense of what you are investigating as you go along.

See the next page for some tips from students on what to consider when recording your findings:

Always note down page numbers for anything you've read — even if it seems unimportant — it may become vital later on.

It can be a real pain having to transcribe interviews from a recording, so I take my own notes as I do the interview and use the recording as a back-up to clarify anything I've missed.

I was observing people's habits in airport departure lounges — I started by writing long descriptions of what everyone did but soon found I could use tables to record a tally and make brief notes.

I had to do case studies based on my professional placements. It was easier to keep track of what I did by writing a diary entry each day than trying to remember it all at the end of the week.

Our lecturer used to collect in our lab books at the end of each practical class so we couldn't mess around and forget to fill them in later.

I learned from a few late-night panics to always record the full bibliographical details of everything you read and keep your references up to date as you go along!

A lab technician threw out my soil samples — total nightmare. I was able to salvage something as I'd kept a record of what I'd found so far and notes on what each sample held. I was able to describe what I would have found out and get marks anyway.

Writing up as you go along

People often mistakenly think that because a report is an account of an investigation, it can only be written up *after* you have finished conducting the investigation. However, research is unpredictable, potentially open-ended, and doesn't often go in a neat linear direction … so waiting until you have completely finished before writing up may leave you with little or no time left.

Writing up sooner rather than later will help you clarify your thinking and identify any gaps in your investigation that you need to fill with more reading or research. It breaks up the writing process, and avoids having an overwhelming task at the end.

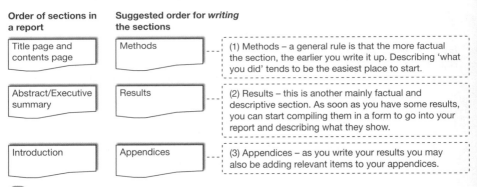

Order of sections in a report

Title page and contents page

Abstract/Executive summary

Introduction

Suggested order for *writing* the sections

Methods

Results

Appendices

(1) Methods – a general rule is that the more factual the section, the earlier you write it up. Describing 'what you did' tends to be the easiest place to start.

(2) Results – this is another mainly factual and descriptive section. As soon as you have some results, you can start compiling them in a form to go into your report and describing what they show.

(3) Appendices – as you write your results you may also be adding relevant items to your appendices.

Methods	Introduction	(4) Introduction – sections that explain and develop the purpose of the research are usually written next. Once you have a clear idea of what you are doing, you can select the most relevant bits of your background reading and refine your aims and questions. This will help you see how to interpret and analyse your findings.
Results	Discussion	(5) Discussion – once you have clarified what you are aiming to find out and what previous investigations have shown, you can use this to help interpret your findings.
Discussion	Conclusion and recommendations	(6) Conclusion – this should follow from your discussion and summarise the important points of your report, plus any recommendations.
Conclusion and recommendations	Abstract/Executive summary	(7) Abstract – this section should be written last, as it's a succinct overview of the whole report.
References	References	(8) References – hopefully you've been compiling these as you go along, but also do a final check through to make sure every source you've referred to in the body of your report is included in your references.
Appendices	Title page and contents page	(9) Contents page and title page – it is usually easiest to compile these as your final task; your redrafting is finished and your page numbers should be fixed.

Adapted from LearnHigher report writing webpages: www.learnhigher.ac.uk/Students/Report-writing.html

Writing up as you go along doesn't necessarily have to be in full sentences or in the best academic style (at this stage!) – it is simply to make your life easier. You can make notes under the relevant headings of your report to expand later. Alternatively, try 'free writing' (write continuously for a set time period, say 10 minutes, without stopping or editing).

Writing up as you go along – it doesn't matter *how* you do it, as long as you do it!

Planning your report

Much of the planning of your report structure is done for you by the report headings – but you still need to plan each section. You need to have a logical order to the information under each heading as well as overall.

Most people plan each report section separately just before they're going to write it. Note down all the points you want to make in that section, look through them, grouping similar points together and discarding irrelevant points, put the points in an order that makes sense – plan done!

3 Structuring your report

A report gives a logical and ordered structure to an investigative process. The sections help the reader know what to expect and find the information they need. As each section of a report does a different job, they each have a different writing style to suit.

This chapter looks at the main sections of a report in turn, explaining their purpose in the overall report, what they should contain, and how they should be written. For each report section the diagram in the margin shows where the section comes in the report structure and the other sections that are related to it.

It is likely that your report will contain some, if not all, of the following sections, but these are just a guide. You should follow the specific instructions given to you by your lecturers, as different academic subjects and professions have their own variations on this structure. (See 'Types of reports' in Chapter 1 for an example of a variation for a business report p. 20.)

Respect the formal structure of reports, but see it as a communication tool, not a set of rigid rules.

What section should this go in?

People tend to be intimidated by the formality of report structures and get anxious about which section information should go in, but if you consider the purpose of your piece of information and its role in your report you will know which section is appropriate:

▶ Does it provide background to your research? (*Introduction*)
▶ Does it describe how you collected evidence? (*Methods*)
▶ Does it present factual data? (*Results*)
▶ Does it analyse the evidence in the context of background reading? (*Discussion*)
▶ Does it summarise key findings and make recommendations for action? (*Conclusion*). (Adapted from University of Reading 2008b.)

> The **introduction** and **discussion** sections are likely to be the longest, contain the most critical analysis … and so be worth the most marks!

Title and contents pages

Professionally produced reports normally have a title page and contents page so the readers know who is responsible for the document and can find information easily. If you are writing a long report for a project or dissertation, you will probably need to include a title page and contents page.

A title page clearly shows your name, your report title, and the date it was completed.

The contents page is an outline of the structure of your report, showing the headings of each section and the pages they start on. A clear, easy-to-read contents page will help your marker understand your structure (and it will put them in a good mood!)

Save time by using **styles** in Word (consistently use Heading 1 style for your main heading, Heading 2 style for sub-headings etc.).

Then you can automatically generate a contents list.

In Word 2007 and 2010, go to **'References'** > 'Table of Contents' and select one of the automatic formats. This will generate your list and page numbers for you – as long as you have used your heading styles consistently.

If you are using Word for Mac 2011, go to **'Document Elements'** > **'Table of Contents'**.

Example contents page for a report

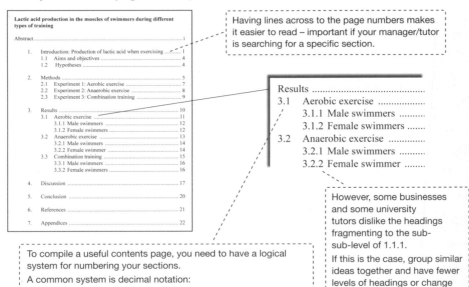

Lactic acid production in the muscles of swimmers during different types of training

Having lines across to the page numbers makes it easier to read – important if your manager/tutor is searching for a specific section.

Results ....
3.1   Aerobic exercise ....
      3.1.1 Male swimmers ....
      3.1.2 Female swimmers ....
3.2   Anaerobic exercise ....
      3.2.1 Male swimmers ....
      3.2.2 Female swimmer ....

However, some businesses and some university tutors dislike the headings fragmenting to the sub-sub-level of 1.1.1.

If this is the case, group similar ideas together and have fewer levels of headings or change Word's table of contents settings to only include level 1 and level 2 headings.

To compile a useful contents page, you need to have a logical system for numbering your sections.

A common system is decimal notation:

- Main headings are numbered in sequence (1, 2, 3).
- The levels of sub-headings under this are numbered after the decimal point: 1.1 for the first level, 1.1.1 for the next level etc.).

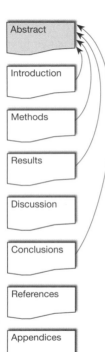

Abstract / Executive summary

This is a concise summary of your whole report. It helps your readers decide whether they want to read the whole report – it acts like your 'shop window'.

Sometimes the abstract or executive summary is the only part of the report that people read, so it has to stand on its own and give a fair and useful reflection of your work.

Abstracts are most commonly found in research reports. They give an overview of the key aims, methods, findings, and conclusions.

As the abstract summarises the whole report, you should write it last. It should be only about 200 words or fewer and is normally written as one paragraph.

It should contain a sentence or two about the

- purpose and aims
- methods used
- main findings
- most important conclusions.

Nurse prescribers' perceptions of their extended professional role

Purpose and aims.

Training in skills such as nurse prescribing has resulted in nurses taking on roles that have traditionally been associated with doctors. Despite the benefits of this greater role, some researchers have been concerned that this may negatively affect nurses' relationships with colleagues. This report investigates whether these views are shared by a group of recently qualified nurse prescribers. Interviews were conducted with a group of 15 nurse prescribers at Eastham Hospital. The interviews were analysed thematically in line with the principles of grounded theory.

Methods used (note they are described very briefly)

Main findings.

The interviews showed that being trained as nurse prescribers complements many aspects of nursing. It helps nurses to adopt a more holistic approach to patient care, and it increases job satisfaction. However, during the interview process the concern about colleagues' lack of understanding of their new role emerged as a consistent theme for nurse prescribers, suggesting that further awareness-raising and training for the whole healthcare team may be needed.

Most important conclusions.

If you find it hard to start writing your abstract, try highlighting the key sentence from each section of your report. Cut and paste these sentences together, then read through and redraft them into a workable abstract.

An executive summary is more commonly found in business reports. Whereas an abstract has an academic focus, an executive summary is very practical. It is usually aimed at those at the higher level of management, and is designed to give them all the information they need to make a decision just based on reading the executive summary.

It too is written last. It can be slightly longer than an abstract (usually about 1 or 2 paragraphs, or a page for longer reports) and can sometimes include bullet points to highlight key recommendations.

It contains a sentence or two about the

▸ key problem
▸ scope and objective of the report
▸ main findings and conclusions
▸ crucial recommendations.

Performance management of Eastham Hospital

With recent budget concerns in the health service, the need to assess performance and accountability in regional hospitals has become even more important. This report was commissioned to assess whether a Balanced Scorecard (BSC) approach to performance management could be used in Eastham Hospital. The BSC tool was seen to be appropriate as it provides an overview of the risks and benefits of strategic and operational decisions. The information gathered from scorecard results will provide a means of accountability and support the health planning process. Based on the willingness of the board and employee attitude, it was concluded that the BSC could be successfully used if the following recommendations are met:

- strengthening communication between senior management and hospital ward teams
- ensuring management are committed to the use of the BSC
- coordinating a target setting and reward system for staff.

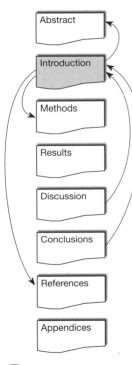

Abstract

Introduction

Methods

Results

Discussion

Conclusions

References

Appendices

Introduction

Your introduction does two main jobs:

1 It introduces the context of your investigation – explains what you have been asked to investigate, why this is important, and how you are going to respond to your brief.

2 It analyses the background literature that relates to your investigation.

The introduction is usually written in an analytical style, comparing and contrasting relevant studies and explaining how other people's previous research is relevant to your investigation.

The extent to which you refer to the background literature depends on the purpose of your report:

- *Business reports* – these often have short introductions and focus more on explaining the reason for commissioning the report and the key issue to be investigated than on analysing background literature.
- *Lab reports* – these are short and concentrate on a single experiment, so you need to refer to the most relevant previous studies.
- *Research reports and projects* – these assess your research skills, so you need to demonstrate wider reading and the ability to place your work in the context of a broader range of background literature. Sometimes longer projects and dissertations have a separate literature review section (see pp. 77–8).

The first few paragraphs of your introduction will put the report in context, explaining why it is needed. It will state the main purpose of the report and show how you plan to respond to the brief.

Context and need for the report.

Clear statement of main audience and purpose for the report.

Propose a new marketing campaign for HomeFarm Foods

The rise in organic food producers over the last decade means that just being able to demonstrate that your food is organic is no longer a unique selling point. As a result, HomeFarm Foods, a previous leader in the organic food market, has seen its market share reduced by 15% (Mintel 2010). The purpose of this report, commissioned by the marketing managers of HomeFarm Foods, is to propose a campaign to regain HomeFarm's dominant position. Young people are eating more ethically and locally produced food (Biz Premier 2011), suggesting this would be a profitable area of expansion for HomeFarm Foods. Therefore, this report will focus on a campaign for HomeFarm's locally sourced seasonal fruit targeted at 16–18-year-olds who are able to influence their parents' purchasing decisions …

In business reports, the background reading you refer to may be market figures and trends rather than purely academic texts.

Responding to the brief by narrowing the focus and justifying this.

Then the introduction should present an analysis of what the background literature says about the topics of the report, and assess the strengths and weaknesses of these previous studies. For example:

> *Investigate the accident reporting mechanisms in a local work place and assess them according to relevant Health and Safety guidelines*
>
> … Skepper's recent study introduces a new model for assessing the dangers of work place injuries (2011). He identifies the overall total damage done as more important than the frequency of injuries (Skepper 2011). However, this model does not fully consider Archer's theory of 'Under-reporting' which states that people are less likely to report frequently occurring small accidents until a critical mass of injuries is reached (2009)…

Only the relevant points of the study and the theory are mentioned briefly – but you need a confident and thorough understanding of the studies first to be able to refer to them so concisely.

Comparing two different approaches and using one study to identify a weakness in the other. **Not simply summarising each study in turn!**

For more example sentences and models for how to refer to your background literature concisely, see the Academic Phrasebank: www.phrasebank.manchester.ac.uk/

The studies you write about in your introduction will be the ones you refer to again in your discussion section to help interpret your results.

If your report has a **hypothesis** or **aims and objectives**, the appropriate place to put these is at the end of the introduction, showing how they have been based on and derived from the previous research.

I am pleased to introduce Patel et al. - you'll be seeing more of them later

Showing how the hypothesis for this experiment has been derived from a previous study.

> *The effects of variations in perspective on the perception of the Schroeder Staircase*
>
> … According to Gregory's (1974) account, if adding increasing amounts of perspective affects the depth interpretation of the figure, then the number of perceptual alterations should reduce and/or the time for which the figure appears in perspective should increase.

The hypothesis – what you expect to happen.

Example from Professor John Harris's report writing guide for the Department of Psychology, University of Reading.

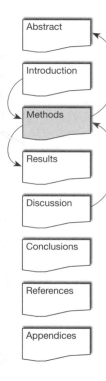

Abstract

Introduction

Methods

Results

Discussion

Conclusions

References

Appendices

Methods

In your methods section you need to describe what you did to conduct your investigation. You need to justify why you chose the methods you did (case studies, interviews, focus groups, experiments etc.).

Normally **business reports** don't include a methods section, as managers are more concerned with *what to do* with the information than *how* it was collected.

As the methods are descriptive and follow a step-by-step procedure of what you did, it is usually a good section to start writing first.

However, don't underestimate the methods section – it can be tricky to get the appropriate level of detail and description. For example, in an experiment measuring people's reaction to

The methods section in Psychology reports is usually split into the following subsections:
- *Participants*
- *Experiment design*
- *Apparatus*
- *Procedure*
Check your course guidelines for what your lecturers want you to include.

images of spiders, it is important to include the distances of the participant from the viewing screen (as this directly affects their perception and sense of threat) but it is not necessary to go into great detail describing the room, desk and chair that were used in the test (as these were the same conditions for all participants and had little influence on the experiment).

The incidence of code-switching in Malaysian university students studying in the UK

Participants were asked to keep a Language Diary for a period of 24 hours in which they recorded all conversations, describing choice of code, topic of the interaction, and role of the principal speaker. The Language Diary, based on Stark's design (1990) was used as it minimises some of the problems associated with other methods, such as observation in which the observer may influence the target behaviour, and questionnaires in which participants may not have enough awareness of their language behaviour to respond to questions on this topic.

[...]

An email request was sent to all first-year Malaysian students at the university. From the 23 respondents, eight participants (two from each faculty) were selected to get a range of arts and science subjects.

> Justifying choice of methods by referring to previous research, and explaining why other methods were not used.

> If you have participants in your research you need to explain who they were, how many, and how you selected them.

Any piece of research needs to be repeatable so someone else reading your methods section is able to use it to replicate your investigation.

Be precise and give exact measurements. Avoid using ambiguous terms like 'test tube 1, test tube 2' that are meaningless out of context.

> *Testing the effect of different temperatures on enzyme activity*
>
> … The 5 test tubes were placed into water baths and left until they reached the required temperatures of 4°C, 25°C, 37°C, 60°C and 90°C respectively. 2ml of 3% hydrogen peroxide was then added to each of these tubes.

Precise measurements.

You need to describe any specific techniques or specialised equipment that you used.

However, no need to say, for instance, that the hydrogen peroxide was added 'using a pipette', as this is standard scientific equipment all scientists would use.

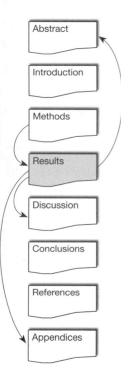

Results

The function of the results section is to describe your results in an orderly way, using both words and appropriate visual mate-

rial (e.g. tables, graphs or diagrams). Label your graphs and tables clearly so you can refer to them easily, and describe the crucial trends and patterns that they show.

You need to describe in words what each table, figure, graph or diagram shows – they won't speak for themselves! (For more on presenting your findings see Chapter 5.)

Usually the order you present your results follows the same order as your research questions or objectives. This provides a logical sequence and links the results back directly to the questions you are trying to answer.

> You can't interpret and present all the data you collect. A good test of whether something is relevant is to return to your aims or research questions and brief – how is what you are presenting going to help answer your brief?

- Present the data in one format only – either a table or graph or diagram. Select the most appropriate form for the trends and comparisons you want to show.
- Pick out for the reader the important *trends* in the data – avoid describing each individual data point in detail.
- Save all *interpretation* of the findings for your discussion section.

The effect of vocal training on acoustic voice quality in primary school teachers.

… Before vocal training, only participant No. 3 was outside the jitter range for a healthy voice (> 1.040% jitter, Boersma & Weenink 2005). As shown in Table 5, all participants demonstrated a reduction in the percentage jitter in their voices following vocal training.

Table 5: Percentage jitter in participants' voices pre- and post-vocal training

Participant no.	Jitter in voice (%)	
	Pre vocal training	**Post vocal training**
1	0.296	0.245
2	0.447	0.213
3	1.198	0.772

The table is clearly labelled with a descriptive title and is referred to in the text.

The main trend in the data.

Only one format for presenting the data.

A table is used, because the measurements up to three decimal places wouldn't be shown so precisely on a bar graph.

Produce a report on the current sources of revenue for the Kings Head Hotel and propose a way of increasing this revenue based on your findings

… Figure 3 shows that room rental provides the largest proportion of revenue for the Kings Head Hotel (43%) followed by drinks sold at the bar (37%). Car park fees make up 23% of the total revenue. The smallest proportion of revenue comes from food sold at the hotel restaurant (7%).

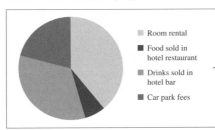

Room rental
Food sold in hotel restaurant
Drinks sold in hotel bar
Car park fees

Figure 3: Proportion of sources of revenue for the Kings Head Hotel in 2011

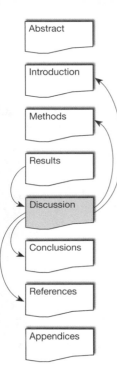

Discussion

This section is where you interpret and explain your results, offering possible reasons why you got the findings you did. It is likely to be one of the longest sections and is written in an explanatory and analytical style.

You need to provide evidence to back up your possible explanations by referring to the previously published studies you analysed in your introduction section. Do the findings of previous studies offer possible reasons for your own results? Are they similar, or do your results depart from them – why might this be?

Using an international real estate firm as a case study, compile a research report analysing the links between financial services and real estate services in global cities

… Hartfield and Wakeman are located near other real estate firms and financial service providers in the three global cities analysed in this report. This seems to support the advantages of agglomeration discussed by Clark (2002) and Taylor et al. (2003). However, it is difficult to identify whether real estate firms move to match the location of financial service firms, or vice versa, because of the general attractiveness of the cities sampled; the choice of office site may be influenced by the broad benefits of the city locations as opposed to specific benefits of agglomeration.

Research suggests decentralisation and agglomeration occur separately and independently (Taylor et al. 2003; Lizeri 2009). Yet when the two processes are analysed together in the case of Hartfield and Wakeman (see Figure 4), it appears that they occur at the same time. This may be due to the processes happening even more rapidly today due to the need to respond to an unstable and changing economic situation.

The example on the previous page uses tentative language like:

▶ 'This seems to support …'
▶ 'It appears that …'
▶ 'This may be due to …'

This is often called **academic hedging.**

A possible explanation for the results might be that…

It is not simply 'sitting on the fence' or being vague; using words like 'may', 'might' or 'possibly' shows that you are aware you cannot give a definitive answer but you are attempting to explain your findings within the limitations of what you have investigated. The causation of your results may not be clear, there may be a number of possible explanations for your findings, or your findings cannot be widely generalised, so using tentative language is appropriate.

For more examples of academic hedging in explaining results, see the Academic Phrasebank: www.phrasebank.manchester.ac.uk/

The discussion is the appropriate place to **raise any limitations** or problems you faced and assess to what extent these shortcomings affected your results. You may also suggest how the limitations could be overcome if the investigation was repeated or developed.

Clear statement of limitations.

Is short-term memory and recall affected by an increase in age?

There were two main limitations with this experiment. One limitation was that there were not enough participants in the over 50 years old age group to make a valid comparison with the other age groups. The second limitation was that the memory task (recalling strings of words) and the laboratory setting were artificial, so did not reflect the kinds of short-term memorising and recall used in 'real life' situations. This indicates that the findings from this experiment cannot necessarily be generalised to explain how memory operates in everyday life. If a more extensive study were carried out, tests that more accurately simulate 'real life' memory operations should be used.

How the limitations affected the results.

What could be done to overcome the limitations.

In some business reports the discussion section might not be discussing results but instead analysing information gathered in order to assess a course of action or a particular problem. (See 'What if your report has a different structure?' pp. 71–2.)

Should ColaMax sponsor the building of a new skate park in Littleton?

Risks:

The main risk associated with this project is cost. The starting costs of creating the skate park are high (see Table 2) and there is a risk of losing money if not enough people join the skate club, or if partnerships with local schools are not found.

A further risk is the perception of the skate park by Littleton residents. If the park is regarded as a cause of antisocial behaviour then ColaMax may be negatively associated with this behaviour.

Benefits:

A crucial benefit of the project is the location within the catchment area of four secondary schools with a total population of 8,400 students (Littleton Borough Council 2010). This offers a wide range of users and potential joint initiatives with the schools and local clubs …

As opposed to strengths and weaknesses, business reports may instead refer to 'risks' and 'benefits'.

Sub-headings to break down the analysis of the problem.

If you are writing a business report for an imaginary client, you may be expected to refer to figures, company data or statistics as opposed to academic texts in your discussion.

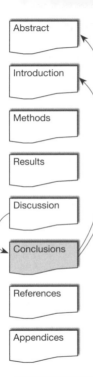

Abstract

Introduction

Methods

Results

Discussion

Conclusions

References

Appendices

Conclusions and recommendations

This section sums up the key points you have made – it is a short section and it doesn't introduce any new information.

> *I get irritated with conclusions that end with 'further research is needed'. Further research is always needed – tell me what specifically needs to be researched and why.*
> *(Psychology lecturer)*

Usually a lab or research report will just have conclusions, but a report aimed at a real or imaginary client is likely to ask for recommendations as well.

Conclusions

- Look backwards to the original brief and summarise the main findings of your investigation.
- Let your readers know **why your findings are important**.
- Give the crucial 'take-away' message that you want to leave your readers with.
- Include any suggestions for further research if appropriate.

The conclusion is the section where you ask yourself **'So what'?**

So what do my findings show and *so what* does this mean for my readers – why should they care?

This helps you see the wider context and see the contribution that your investigation has made to our understanding of the topic.

Relationship between hand, wrist and forearm circumferences and maximal grip strength

This experiment has shown that of all the data measured (hand, wrist and forearm circumference), hand circumference presented the strongest correlation with maximal grip strength. The correlation between hand circumference and maximal grip strength was evident in both male and female participants and for both non-dominant and dominant hands. Using hand circumference alone it is possible to predict maximal grip strength in adults. Given the suggested relationship between maximal grip strength and overall muscle mass, hand circumference may be a valuable indicator of general muscle health in adults.

Brief summary of the main findings – relating back to the original brief.

Clear statement of the 'take-away' message of the investigation.

Answering the 'so what' question – why we should care about these findings and their wider implications.

Recommendations

▶ Look forward and suggest specific actions that should be taken as a result of your investigation.
▶ Let your readers know **what they should do based on your findings**.
▶ State the crucial changes you want your readers to make.

Bullet points are used to make each recommendation stand out.

Consistency in use of tense and grammatical construction for each recommendation.

Investigate whether the Students Union should continue to hold a local produce market each week

Following the student survey and financial analysis, it is recommended that:

- The Union switches the market from once a week on a Friday lunchtime to every 2 weeks on a Wednesday lunchtime.
- The Manager of the Union liaises with local farmers to get a wider selection of produce for sale.
- The Union Sabbatical Officers run a cooking competition to promote the market in Spring term.

Specific – it identifies *who* is responsible for the action and *when* they should do it.

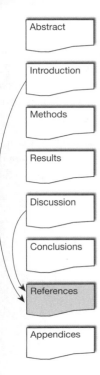

Abstract

Introduction

Methods

Results

Discussion

Conclusions

References

Appendices

References

The references section comes next and it contains the full list of any works you have referred to in the body of your report.

It is a good idea to compile your reference list as you go along so you can keep track of all your sources and avoid any last-minute panic – but do a final check during the proofreading stage to make sure all sources referenced in the body of your report appear in your reference list and vice versa.

Appendices

The appendices come last in your report and contain any additional information that is useful for your reader. This may include raw data, example questionnaires, interview transcripts – things which would be disruptive to your reader to include in full in the body of the report.

However, the appendices are not a general dumping-ground for everything else you have collected during the course of your investigation! Each item needs to be selected and have a purpose.

Make sure you *refer* to the items in your appendices or your readers won't know they're there. Appendices are arranged in the order that they are referred to in your report. Label each appendix, and briefly refer the reader to it in the body of your report. For example, 'See Appendix A for the interview questions'. Put each appendix on a new page and don't forget to add the heading 'Appendices' and relevant starting page number to your contents list if you have one.

What if your report has a different structure?

What if your investigation doesn't fit the 'introduction, methods, results, discussion, conclusion' model? Many **business reports** don't follow this format because companies often have their own report templates, and because business reports need to be flexible and respond directly to the needs of the client and brief.

If you have not been given a report structure by your lecturer, you need to create your own headings based on your brief.

Start from your brief and break it down into sub-questions, or separate issues, that you need to investigate – these could form the basis of your headings. Group similar sub-questions or ideas together and find a sensible order for the headings that leads the reader through your investigation step by step.

Your headings need to be meaningful and descriptive, giving your readers a clear idea of the purpose and contents of each section.

Imagine you are given the following brief:

> Investigate the feasibility of relocating Gino's Café to outside the city centre

The following headings would work well:

1 Executive Summary
2 Reasons for proposed move
  2.1 Rising rent prices in the city centre
  2.2 Need for a larger venue
  2.3 Increased competition of cafés in city centre
3 Finding an appropriate new location
4 Renovating new premises
5 Relocation of employees
6 Marketing and creating a new clientele
7 Financial implications of moving
8 Conclusions and recommendations
9 References

Acts like an introduction – establishes the purpose of the report, why it's needed and gives important background context.

Descriptive headings. The report sections break down the issues related to the relocation and deal with each in turn.

Financial section comes just before the conclusions as it is derived from an analysis of all the other sections. Also, it is a crucial section, so it's easier for the reader to see at the end.

4 Business plans, project proposals and dissertations

Business plans, project proposals and dissertations share many of the features of reports, such as a formal structure divided by headings. However, since they have different purposes to fulfil there are some differences between these assignment formats and reports.

Business plans

Like other types of reports, business plans have a target audience and purpose; they are persuasive documents designed to attract investors or collaborators. If you are being asked to write a business plan for an assignment, you need to convince your imaginary (or real) investors that you have a clear, realistic, financially workable idea.

The structure of business plans depends on the needs of your proposed business idea and the needs of your potential investors, but they usually cover the following areas:

- *Executive summary* – An overview to encourage your investors to continue reading

- *Company description* – Background on your company, its aims and plans for the future
- *Management and organisation* – How your company is organised, the main members of the management team and their experience
- *Market and competition* – Your research into the other products or services available in your market
- *Product or service* – What you are offering and what is the unique selling point – how will you distinguish yourself from your competitors?
- *Marketing and sales* – How you will promote your product or service and ensure sales
- *Financial information* – The most important section and what investors are concerned about – it needs to be robust and consider initial capital, expenditure and projected income.

For more on business plans see Marsen (2007).

Project proposals

> *Many students describe viable ideas in their business plans but don't get good marks because they fail to give detailed financial information – no investor would stand for that!*
>
> *(Management lecturer)*

If you are doing a longer piece of research like a dissertation, you will probably have to submit a proposal before you can get started. The proposal is a chance for you to present information on:

- *what* **you want to research** (an explanation of your topic and research questions)
- *why* **this is important** (the rationale behind your project, based on your initial background reading)
- *how* **you will research it** (a summary of your methods and a time plan breaking down the stages of your investigation).

A report normally doesn't include a time plan, as the research has already been conducted and your audience cares about what you found out, not about how long it took.

However, a significant part of your proposal will be a project plan, breaking down your investigation into main stages and allocating an amount of time for each stage.

Your tutor wants to see that you have a realistic plan for completing your investigation in the available time.

A report is about the *past*: you are reporting on what you *have done*. A report is therefore mostly written in the past tense.

A proposal is about the *future*: you are justifying what you *will do*. It is, therefore, appropriate to write your proposal mostly in the future tense, e.g. 'This project will investigate …'; 'Focus groups will be conducted …'

Projects and dissertations

If you are doing a dissertation in a science or social science subject and you are collecting your own data (e.g. conducting interviews, questionnaires, experiments etc.), it is likely your dissertation will have a report structure:

- Introduction
- Literature review
- Methods
- Results
- Discussion
- Conclusions.

> *In a dissertation you'll be dealing with far more references than normal, so using reference managing software like Endnote or RefMan can help. It can take a little getting used to, but saves time in the long run.*
> (Meteorology lecturer)

Your dissertation is like an extended report with each section forming its own chapter.

The main difference between a report and a dissertation (apart from length!) is that a dissertation often has a separate chapter for analysing the background literature – the **literature review**.

The literature review comes after the very brief introduction chapter. It is *not* an historical narrative of past research, nor a summary of everything you have read.

Instead, you are comparing and contrasting previous research in your field, analysing the strengths and weaknesses of these studies and identifying what this tells you about your own project.

A literature review chapter usually has sub-headings to help you structure it and help you avoid retelling a narrative of what you have read.

Look at what themes or main issues are coming from your background reading – use these themes to help group your reading together. You could use colour coding or do spidergrams to identify the studies or research that relates to the same theme.

<table>
<tr>
<td>

Spidergrams are good for bringing together lots of research and for creative thinking.

You're not constrained by a linear list and you can make links and connections easily.

</td>
<td>

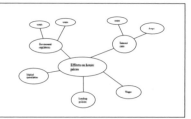

</td>
</tr>
</table>

Once you have grouped your reading under headings, compare and contrast the studies under each heading, analysing their methods and findings and always showing how these findings relate to your own investigation.

For more on dissertations see Greetham (2009).

Reports are as much about visual communication as they are about written communication. Much of the meaning in a report is conveyed through its formal structure: headings, lists and bullet points; and through presentation of findings: tables, graphs and diagrams.

When presenting your results you need to choose the most appropriate way to represent them so that your readers can see the key trends, patterns or themes.

Imagine you are presenting the findings for the following report:

> Does the current university system provide good value for money for students?

You might consider using all or some of the following methods of data presentation, depending on how appropriate they are for the findings you have.

Tables

Good for: presenting exact numbers
Not good for: showing overall trends

> Clearly labelled with a useful descriptive heading.

> Comparing so many different categories would be difficult on a single graph.

> Units of the data also clearly shown.

Table 1: Yearly expenditure for three Brookhampton students (excluding tuition fees)

	Housing	Food	Personal items (clothes, phone etc.)	Socialising	Books, computers, equipment	**TOTAL**
			Expenditure in £			
Student A	4,004	1,589	1,894	1,197	987	**£ 9,671**
Student B	3,569	1,300	900	937	936	**£ 7,642**
Student C	3,400	1,607	1,549	1,402	876	**£ 8,834**

> We scan from top to bottom so it is easy to skim down the table columns and compare all three students' expenditure in the same category.

> We read horizontally from left to right so it is easy to read across the table rows and find the breakdown of expenditure for each student and their total expenditure.

Graphs

You may be using a programme like Microsoft Excel to draw your graphs – but remember that computers can only work with the numbers you give them and can't do your thinking for you. Are you using the appropriate scales and plotting the points accurately?

Line graphs

Good for: showing changes over time or how two variables interact
Not good for: showing precise numbers

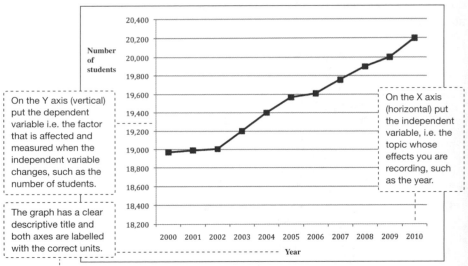

On the Y axis (vertical) put the dependent variable i.e. the factor that is affected and measured when the independent variable changes, such as the number of students.

On the X axis (horizontal) put the independent variable, i.e. the topic whose effects you are recording, such as the year.

The graph has a clear descriptive title and both axes are labelled with the correct units.

Figure 1: Total number of students attending Brookhampton University 2000–2010

Bar charts

Good for: showing comparisons between the total amounts in different categories
Not good for: showing complex multiple comparisons on a single graph

Two bars in each category should really be the limit, as further bars make the chart too complex and it is hard to compare across categories.

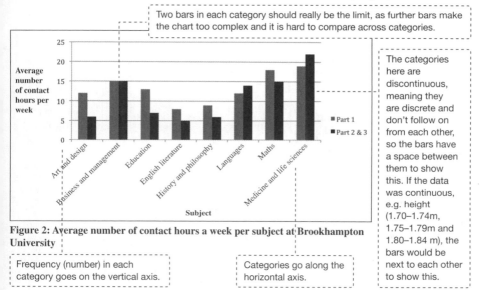

Figure 2: Average number of contact hours a week per subject at Brookhampton University

The categories here are discontinuous, meaning they are discrete and don't follow on from each other, so the bars have a space between them to show this. If the data was continuous, e.g. height (1.70–1.74m, 1.75–1.79m and 1.80–1.84 m), the bars would be next to each other to show this.

Frequency (number) in each category goes on the vertical axis.

Categories go along the horizontal axis.

Pie charts

Good for: showing large-scale relative proportions

Not good for: showing the size of the whole 'cake', total figures or fine differences in proportions

Not too many segments. More than 5 or 6 segments becomes difficult for the reader to interpret.

Large, distinct segments. If the segments are too small or too close to each other in size it is hard to distinguish between them – consider using a table or bar chart instead.

A pie chart can't show the total number of students – we don't know if there are 90 or 90,000 students! So if you are using pie charts to show proportion of budgets, remember that we also need to know the overall budget total as well!

Clear key showing what each segment represents.

Pie charts usually need to be in colour; it is hard to see the difference between segments and read the key if they are just shades of grey.

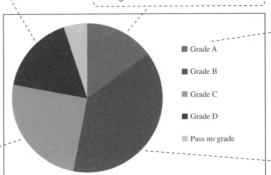

- Grade A
- Grade B
- Grade C
- Grade D
- Pass no grade

Figure 3: Proportion of final degree classifications for Brookhampton students graduating in 2010

Photographs

Good for: illustrating what things look like in 'real life'
Not good for: detailed and precise technical representations

Although photos are aesthetically pleasing, it can be difficult to see what is being represented and why. The angle of the shot, the sharpness of focus, the light source and the quality of the photo's reproduction can all distort or obscure what you are trying to show. If you are trying to show detail, a simple line drawing may be better.

If you have collected many photographs, for example from fieldwork, it may be more appropriate to include a relevant (clearly titled and labelled) selection in an appendix.

When including any photograph, ask yourself what purpose it has in the report and whether your report would be affected if it wasn't there.
(Geography and Environmental Science lecturer)

Diagrams

Good for: representing complex processes or detailed information in visual form
Not good for: showing 'real life' three-dimensional perspectives

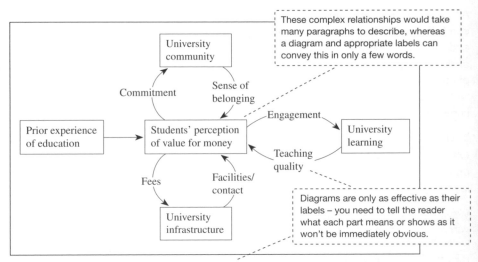

Figure 4: Factors influencing students' perception of the value for money of university

Diagrams that are too small or poorly reproduced will frustrate your reader. Reports are professional documents, so the visual information needs to be presented to a high standard. Make use of the services and expertise at your university (IT services, lab technicians, librarians, graphic designers) to help you present the information in the form you want.

If a diagram is worth including, then it's worth going large! (Graphic designer and tattoo artist)

Maps and plans

Good for: showing spatial representations and geographical locations
Not good for: showing 'real life' three-dimensional perspectives

Every map or plan should have a scale marked in metric units at the bottom. Maps conventionally represent north as the top of the page and have a compass arrow showing this.

If your plan or map uses symbols or shading to represent features in the landscape, you need to have a key interpreting what these symbols show. It is good practice to incorporate your key in the map (usually over to one side) rather than separate from, or underneath, your map. This prevents the key becoming lost or disconnected from your map when you format your report.

Interviews and observations

When presenting qualitative data gained through interviews or observations, you need a systematic way of sorting through all the words you have collected – usually this is done by grouping similar ideas into themes.

For more detail of this method, see Thomas G (2011) *Doing Research* in this series.

Once you have identified your main themes and grouped your findings under these themes you need to present them in your report in tables or as quotations.

Table 2: What do you think constitutes 'value for money' when it comes to your university experience?

Theme	Response	Interviewee
Availability of staff	'It's no good my tutor only being available for one hour a week – they should provide a better service.'	Interviewee no. 2
	'My dissertation tutor was really helpful to start with, then he went on research leave – we were abandoned with no explanation.'	Interviewee no. 5
	'I understand staff are busy, but my lecturer makes time to go through our feedback. She treats us like individuals.'	Interviewee no. 6
Sense of belonging	'I commute in from home – I feel like I'm paying full price but only getting half the experience.'	Interviewee no. 5
	'It is the best experience – where else would I get the chance to do so much and meet so many people – I don't want to leave!'	Interviewee no. 4

Tables are useful for comparing responses to a question at a glance without having to write a long description of the reply from each interviewee.

You can include short quotations in the table as evidence of the responses under each theme.

Organise the table thematically.

For more in-depth analysis you may wish to select one or two longer quotations as typical examples.

Students from Arts and Humanities subjects generally felt their fees were not directly funding their course:

> It doesn't take much to buy a few books for an English class. I think our fees just subsidise the expensive equipment for science students. (Interviewee no. 3)

As shown by interviewee 3, students are more alert to ideas of fairness in how universities allocate their budgets.

These longer quotations are often indented in the text or in a textbox to highlight them in the body of your report.

Ensure you analyse each quotation that you include.

Labelling your tables and figures

Tables and figures are labelled separately and consecutively in the order they appear in the text:

Table 1
Figure 1
Figure 2
Figure 3
Figure 4
Table 2

The label for a table goes on top (a table cloth goes on top of a table) and the label for a figure goes below (a figure needs something to stand on).

Include a brief descriptive title explaining what the table or figure shows – you don't need to write 'A graph showing …' or 'A diagram showing …' – we can see it is a graph or diagram.

The title needs to be meaningful and precise. Compare the difference between the following titles:

'Figure 5: Student costs'

and

'Figure 5: Average student living costs, 1995–2010'

When you refer to the table or figure in your text put the relevant table or figure number in brackets: 'Student living costs increased at a steady rate in line with inflation, until recently when high rent prices have caused a sharp increase in total costs (see Figure 5).'

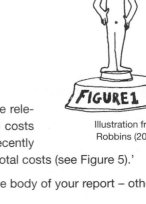

Illustration from Robbins (2009)

It is important to refer to all your tables and figures in the body of your report – otherwise there is no point in them being there!

Referencing unusual sources

If you include data, tables, diagrams, graphs or photographs taken from other sources in your report, you need to show where you got them from by referencing them.

Be consistent in how you reference these sources, and include enough information so that someone else can find them again.

There are good comprehensive style guides online, such as these Harvard referencing examples from Staffordshire University: www.staffs.ac.uk/about_us/university_departments/information_services/learning_support/refzone/harvard/

Here are some examples of how to reference more unusual sources. Like any source, you have to:

▶ give the in-text reference (or citation)
▶ give the full reference in the references section.

Images (graphs, diagrams, photographs, drawings)

In your text	In your references
The representation of the common cold virus by Khan (2007, in Fish 2008) shows …	Khan S (2007). Common Cold Virus. In Fish G (ed.), *Medical Virology* (4th edition, 2008). London: Kings Medical Press.

You need to show who created the image and when, but also where you found this diagram if it was reprinted in a book or on a website.

Interviews

In your text	In your references
Dowling (2010) stated that wikis were an effective way for social workers in different offices to share information ...	Dowling B (2010). *Use of wikis to create a community of practice amongst social workers.* [Interview] West Berkshire Council offices, Reading. Conducted by L Lilani. 27 October 2010.

Maps

In your text	In your references
As can be seen on the map of the Peak District (Ordnance Survey 2011) ...	Ordnance Survey (2011). *OS Explorer Map of the Peak District: Dark Peak Area.* Scale 1:25 000. Southampton: Ordnance Survey.
In Cardiff city centre, the building of the Millennium Stadium has led to urban regeneration (Google Maps 2011).	Google Maps (2011). Cardiff City Centre: Castle Street District. No scale. http://maps.google.com/maps?q =Millenium+Stadium,+cardiff&hl=en&ll=51.479071 [accessed 23 September 2011].

Reports are informative and they have a purpose, so if the writing is unclear or irrelevant the effectiveness of the information is lost and the purpose is not achieved.

This is especially true in a work environment where clear, incisive communication is a powerful tool for persuasion and achieving change. A poorly written report will be ignored or dismissed – both you and your message will lose authority. At university, a poorly written report will also lose you marks!

Write concisely – it's easy to say, but how can you achieve this?

Write to express not to impress!

The best academic writing explains complex ideas in a clear and straightforward way.

You need to use appropriate words – don't try to make your writing appear more advanced by substituting longer, more difficult words when simple ones work best.

If you use a thesaurus to find more 'academic-sounding', words here's what you might end up with:

The contemporary transportation profusion has been instigated by the Council appointing road works concomitantly as a construction enterprise is entitled to commence.

… when what you really meant to write was:

The current traffic congestion has been caused by the Council scheduling road works at the same time as a building project is due to start.

Selecting alternative words from a thesaurus can distort what you mean to say and lose marks. Have confidence in your own way of expressing your ideas – this will be more genuine and direct.

The current traffic profusion is being investigated THESAURUS

Use technical terms appropriately

Each academic subject has its own technical terms and shared vocabulary – and you need to use these specialist terms appropriately and accurately.

If there is a correct term, use it! Don't substitute it for another similar word for the sake of variety. For example 'IQ' and 'intelligence' don't mean the same thing.

Use the right words for your audience. If you are writing a report for sports science professionals they will understand the term 'aerobic capacity'. However, if your report is for a local running club, a more appropriate explanation might be, 'the ability to process oxygen for conversion to energy'.

Specialist vocabulary usually has its own abbreviations and acronyms. It is good practice to use the full name the first time it appears in your report with the abbreviation or acronym in brackets. For example: Cognitive Behavioural Therapy (CBT). After that you should just use the shortened version.

Use words with accuracy and precision

The example texts below contain many common problems:

Subjective and overly elaborate description – better to use 'bright red' or 'light pink'.

Lack of accurate evidence to support a claim. Which book? No reasons are given for *why* the results were unexpected.

After adding the solution, the mixture in the test tube went a vivid scarlet red, which was unexpected, as this was not the same as the washed-out pink colour it was supposed to go according to the book. The test tube was then shaken and left for a while in the test tube stand. After a few days, the mixture had settled to the bottom and dried out, which was not supposed to have happened; this was a bit of a problem.

Vague term - how long exactly?

Imprecise term. How many days? Use specific figures, e.g. 'three days' or '70 hours'.

Ambiguous and overly informal – what *exactly* was the problem and why?

> The results show that 85% of students who recycle more than 50% of their rubbish are involved in volunteering or charity activities. This is significant as it shows that students who recycle more are better people who make a much more valuable contribution to our society.

Be careful about imprecise use of 'significant' in reference to findings – do you mean 'important' or 'statistically significant'?

Not objective – what is meant by 'better' or 'valuable contribution'? The author is allowing personal bias to influence their explanations.

Vague – much more than whom? Need to show who this group is being compared to!

Use of first person

Reports are formal academic writing so they are usually written in the **third person** and using the **passive voice.**

Passive voice

I interviewed six marketing managers

This is an active sentence because the subject (I) is doing the action (interviewing) to the object of the sentence (marketing managers).

However, in a formal academic report, the sentence would become:

Six marketing managers were interviewed.

This uses the passive voice because there is no direct subject to do the action. Instead, the action (interviewed) is done to the object (marketing managers).

Thus,

I conducted five focus groups with first year students

becomes

*Five focus groups with first year students **were conducted***.

This is an artificial way of writing, as we know that investigations don't just happen on their own – someone is responsible for doing them. However, since your readers are interested in *what was done* and not *who was doing it*, the passive voice focuses attention on the process and evidence, and minimises the temptation to include unsupported personal opinions.

The exception is if you are writing a reflective report in which your evidence is based on your personal experiences or observations, for example reporting on a professional placement. Then the authority of your evidence comes from your own professional viewpoint. You need to show that you have reflected and learned from these experiences, so it is appropriate to write in the first person.

For example: 'I intended the quick start to the lesson to be engaging, but I noticed that the pupils were soon becoming restless as they did not know what was coming next. In future, I need to use clear "advance organisers" (Ausubel 1960) to alert the class to the key parts of the lesson.'

For more on reflective writing, see Williams K (2012) *Reflective Writing* in this series.

Use of tenses

In a report, you are reporting what *has happened* so you will be writing mostly in the past tense, especially when describing your methods.

However, there is an exception: you write in the present tense when discussing what your own and other people's findings show. This is because the explanations for your findings (and those of other people's research) are applicable *now*.

▶ When you are describing what was done and what was found (in your own investigation and other people's research), **use the past tense**, as you are reporting what has happened.
▶ When you are stating what the findings show and what can be concluded from them (in your own and other people's research), **use the present tense**, as you are reporting knowledge that is applicable now.

> Kahmen et al. (2005) claim that *T. inodorum* has a high ability to recover from stress caused by drought. However, in this experiment, the reproductive development of the *T. inodorum* decreased when it was subjected to drought conditions. This result suggests that despite being able to recover quickly, drought has a lasting effect on the plant's growth and future development.

Present tense – summarising what other people's findings show.

Past tense – describing what you did and what you found.

Present tense – stating what your findings show.

Cutting unnecessary words

Planning each section of your report before writing it will help you stay on track. Also, allocate approximate word counts for each section based on your overall word limit. Having a target to stick to avoids writing far too much and the painful process of cutting it all out later.

But you can only really make your report concise in the redrafting stage once you have a more distanced, objective view … so leave yourself enough time for a ruthless redraft!

Each section of a report has its own pitfalls that encourage waffling, so ask yourself:

▶ **Introduction and discussion**: Is all the literature I refer to specifically relevant to my investigation?

▶ **Methods**: Have I described my investigation in *enough* detail for someone to replicate it, but not in too much detail?

▶ **Results**: Are all the findings I describe relevant to answering my brief, aims or research questions?

The most common section that students waffle in is the Results, where there's a temptation to explain every single data point rather than trends or relationships.
(Engage in research: www.engageinresearch.ac.uk)

Tighten up your writing by removing unnecessary words or phrases. Print your report out on paper and go through it with a highlighter pen marking any words that could be cut; then read it again to ensure it still makes sense without those additional words. Could you express something using one word instead of several?

What words would you cut from this extract?

> However, unfortunately with the upturn in prices, fewer arable producers will be tempted to venture towards any sort of collaborative farming other than 'buying groups'. A sudden downturn in prices may in fact force farmers into some kind of collaborative farming agreement. Although, actually by the time this comes about it may be too little, too late for many farm businesses.

REPORT WRITING

Checking and proofreading

A report is a professional document produced for an audience, so it needs to be accurate and well presented.

When planning your report, leave enough time at the end for the final checks and proofreading.

Proofreading tips

- Leave your report for at least a day before reading it through for the final time.
- Print it out on paper – you can spot mistakes more easily on paper than on screen.
- Read your report aloud – this forces you to read what you actually wrote, not what you *thought* you wrote.
- Read through once for content; then read through again to spot typos.
- Make sure all the texts you referred to are included in your reference list.
- Check (and double-check) any calculations, statistics, graphs etc.

Report writing checklist

Have you ...	Check ✔
Answered the brief?	
Targeted your report at your audience and addressed their purpose for wanting the report written?	
Identified what you needed to find out in order to answer your brief?	
Introduced your investigation and placed it in the context of previous research?	
Ensured all the previous research is relevant to your investigation?	
Described the methods for conducting your investigation fully so someone else could carry it out (if appropriate for your type of report)?	
Presented your results in the most appropriate format?	
Described what your results show in words?	
Made sure the results you present are all relevant for answering your brief?	
Discussed your findings, offering explanations based on the previous research you have read?	

Summed up your key findings in your conclusion?	
Made clear recommendations if appropriate?	
Written an abstract or executive summary summing up your whole report if the brief requires it?	
Compiled your reference list?	
Checked that all texts you refer to are included in your reference list?	
Edited and proofread your report to ensure it is concise and accurate?	
Checked any calculations or statistics if appropriate?	
Checked all figures, diagrams, tables, photos or graphs are correctly labelled, and are referred to in the body of your report?	
Put any additional material in your appendices, labelled them, and referred to them in the body of your report?	
Checked all headings and formatting are accurate and consistent?	
Created a contents page and checked that it is accurate?	

Report writing at work

Once you leave university, the good news is you'll probably never have to write an essay again! But reports are a universal form of presenting information, so it is likely you will be writing reports in your chosen career.

The skills you develop while conducting investigations and writing reports at university are highly valued by employers:

- problem solving
- project management
- team work
- clear, persuasive communication.

It irritates me when someone has just followed the company report template without thinking about what they're communicating.
(Director, software company)

Differences between academic and work reports

Your experience of report writing at university is good preparation, but note there are some important differences from writing reports in a work environment:

Reports at university	Reports at work
Layout and structure	
Your tutors specify the structure and layout they want you to follow.	Many companies and public sector organisations have their own report templates. You need to follow the template, but you still need to *think* about what you are trying to communicate to your readers.
Audience and purpose	
Your main audience is your tutor. If you submit a late or a poor report, it only really affects you.	Your report may have multiple readers, some of whom may be paying your contract or affecting the success of your employers. You have a direct responsibility to address the needs of your readers – on time and on budget!
Use of evidence	
You need to demonstrate knowledge of academic research and theories. You also need to reference these correctly using an appropriate academic referencing style.	You still need to have evidence to support your findings. It probably won't be academic theories, but more 'practical' evidence like sales figures, company documents or feasibility studies.

Reports at university	Reports at work
Authority and expertise	
You gain the respect of your tutor by reading widely and engaging in the course. A well-written report will gain you marks.	You gain authority through your understanding of the company's and client's situations and the expertise you demonstrate. A well-written report will enable people to act on the information you supply.

Employers want graduates who can see their way through a problem, evaluate solutions, and make strong recommendations – your report is how you communicate this process and encourage people to take action based on your expertise.

If you can write good reports, you can make real changes!

A main shortcoming of my graduate employees is they present me with tables and figures in reports but they don't explain what these show; they just expect me magically to know why they are significant.

(Laser physicist)

References

CETL-AURS and University of Reading (2007). *Engage in Research*. Available at www.engageinresearch.ac.uk (accessed 10 January 2012).

Greetham B (2009). *How to write your undergraduate dissertation*. Basingstoke: Palgrave Macmillan.

Marsen S (2007). *Professional writing: the complete guide for business, industry and IT* (2nd edition). Basingstoke: Palgrave Macmillan.

RMIT University (2007). *Differences between essays, reports and journals*. Available at www.dlsweb.rmit.edu.au/lsu/content/2_AssessmentTasks/assess_pdf/diffbet_reportsessays.pdf (accessed 10 January 2012).

Robbins S (2009). *Science study skills*. Basingstoke: Palgrave Macmillan.

University of Reading (2008a). *Features of good reports*. Available at www.reading.ac.uk/internal/studyadvice/StudyResources/Essays/sta-featuresreports.aspx (accessed 10 January 2012).

University of Reading (2008b). *Structuring your report*. Available at www.reading.ac.uk/internal/studyadvice/StudyResources/Essays/sta-structuringreport.aspx (accessed 10 January 2012).

Useful sources

LearnHigher (2011). *Report writing*. Available at www.learnhigher.ac.uk/Students/Report-writing.html (accessed 10 January 2012).

Manchester Metropolitan University and LearnHigher (2008). *Analyse this!!!* Available at www.learnhigher.ac.uk/analysethis/index.html (accessed 10 January 2012).

Staffordshire University (n.d.). *Harvard referencing examples.* Available at www.staffs.ac.uk/about_us/university_departments/information_services/learning_support/refzone/harvard/ (accessed 10 January 2012).

Thomas G (2011). *Doing research*. Basingstoke: Palgrave Macmillan.

University of Kent (2010). *ASK: assignment survival kit*. Available at www.kent.ac.uk/uelt/ai/ask/index.php (accessed 10 January 2012).

University of Manchester (2005). *Academic phrasebank*. Available at www.phrasebank.manchester.ac.uk/ (accessed 10 January 2012).

Williams K (2012). *Reflective writing*. Basingstoke: Palgrave Macmillan.

Index

POCKET STUDY SKILLS
Julia Copus

BRILLIANT WRITING TIPS FOR STUDENTS

POCKET STUDY SKILLS
Janet Godwin

PLANNING YOUR ESSAY

POCKET STUDY SKILLS
Jeanne Godfrey

WRITING FOR UNIVERSITY

POCKET STUDY SKILLS
Kate Williams, Mary Woolliams and Jane Spiro
REFLECTIVE WRITING

POCKET STUDY SKILLS
Kate Williams
GETTING CRITICAL

POCKET STUDY SKILLS
Kate Williams & Jude Carroll
REFERENCING & UNDERSTANDING PLAGIARISM

POCKET STUDY SKILLS

STUDYING WITH DYSLEXIA

Janet Godwin

POCKET STUDY SKILLS

SCIENCE STUDY SKILLS

Sue Robbins

POCKET STUDY SKILLS

BLOGS WIKIS PODCASTS & MORE

Andy Pulman

POCKET STUDY SKILLS
STUDY SKILLS
14 DAYS TO EXAM SUCCESS
...ecker

POCKET STUDY SKILLS
SUCCESS IN GROUPWORK
Peter Hartley & Mark Bacsou

POCKET STUD...
...ry Thomas
DOING RESEARCH

POCKET STUDY SKILLS
Jeanne Godfrey
READING AND MAKING NOTES